# Tilda's
# WINTER
# IDEAS

David and Charles
www.rucraft.co.uk

# Preface

Christmas is not the same without a nice Christmas workshop with family and friends. From experience I know it's wise to plan ahead and send invitations to the workshop before the most intense Christmas shopping begins. That way everybody can relax and enjoy.

In this book you will find ideas for decorations and gifts – large and small sewing projects like different Santas, Christmas stockings and angels that you can make with your friends. Other simple projects like homemade ribbons, soaps and chocolate gifts are suitable for a more impromptu workshop.

If you want to combine the workshop with food and wine, it might be a good idea to make easy projects that won't require too much effort, like cards and paper decorations.

In this book I chose to use paper wings on some of the figures as they are very small and would be difficult to sew. You will find illustrations for the wings in the back of the book. Instead of paper wings, you could also use little twigs, raffia or buy ready-made wings at a craft store.

Have a fun Christmas!

Tone Finnanger

# Contents

www.pandurohobby.com          www.tildasworld.com

**A DAVID & CHARLES BOOK**
© CAPPELEN DAMM AS 2011
www.cappelendamm.no

Originally published as *Tildas Juleverksted*
First published in the UK in 2011 by F&W Media International, LTD

David & Charles is an imprint of F&W Media International, LTD
Brunel House, Forde Close, Newton Abbot, TQ12 4PU, UK

F&W Media International, LTD is a subsidiary of F+W Media, Inc.
4700 East Galbraith Road, Cincinnati, OH 45236

Tone Finnanger has asserted her right to be identified as author
of this work in accordance with the Copyright, Designs and
Patents Act, 1988.

The author and publisher have made every effort to ensure
that all the instructions in the book are accurate and safe, and
therefore cannot accept liability for any resulting injury, damage
or loss to persons or property, however it may arise.

A catalogue record for this book is available from the British
Library.

ISBN-13: 978-1-4463-0205-7 paperback
ISBN-10: 1-4463-0205-9 paperback

Printed in China by RR Donnelley
for F&W Media International, LTD
Brunel House, Forde Close, Newton Abbot,
TQ12 4PU, UK

10 9 8 7 6 5 4 3

Illustrations: Tone Finnanger
Photography: Sølvi Dos Santos
Styling: Ingrid Skaansar
Book design: Tone Finnanger

F+W Media Inc. publishes high quality books on a wide range
of subjects. For more great book ideas visit: www.rucraft.co.uk

# Stuffed Figures

Avoid cutting out parts for the stuffed figures before you start sewing. Instead, fold the fabric right sides together and draw the figure or the parts for the body using the pattern. Sew along the drawn line.

Cut out the figure, including about 3-4mm (1/8 in) seam allowance and 8-10mm (3/8 in) allowance across the openings. Cut notches next to the seam around inside curves (see Figure A).

It can be a good idea to sew a double seam if it is likely to be under extra pressure when you stuff the shape, like along the neck for the Santas and angels.

Use a wooden stick or something similar to help you turn the figures right sides out. Turn out the arms and legs by pushing the blunt end of the wooden stick towards the tip of the limb (see Figure B).
Start closest to the foot/hand and pull the leg/arm down the wooden stick (see Figure C).
Hold the foot/hand and pull at the same time as you hold at the bottom so the arm/leg is turned inside out (see Figure D). Use the wooden stick to help stuff the parts.

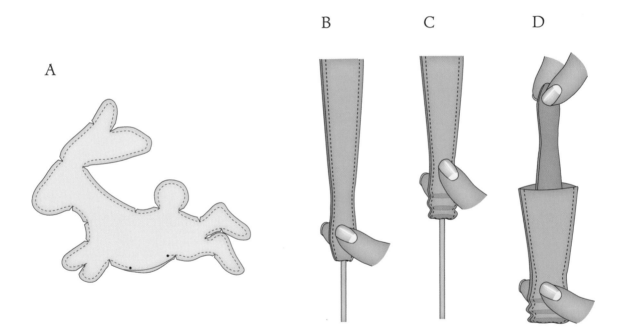

A

B    C    D

## Angel Hair

Start by sewing a fringe across the face with embroidery thread in the same colour as the hair (see Figure A). Attach pins on the forehead and down the middle of the back of the head. Also attach a pin on each side of the head. Twist hair back and forth between the pins on each side and divide it between the pins in the middle (see Figure B). Once the head is covered, stitch the hair down and remove the pins. Make two bundles of hair and attach one to each side of the head (see Figure C).

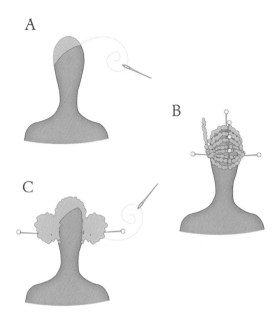

## Faces

Make faces by using pins to find out where the eyes should be. Pull out the pins. Dip the eye tool from the Tilda Face Painting set or the head of a small pin in black paint and stamp on the eyes over the pin holes. Apply Tilda rouge, lipstick or similar with a dry brush to make rosy cheeks.

## Paper Wings

On page 46 you will find patterned wings for the Mini Angel and Winter Bunny. You can scan and print out the wings, or make a copy. For one set of wings you need two copies, four wings all together.
Cut out the four wings and glue them wrong sides together so you have the pattern on both sides of each wing. Attach the wings to the figure using adhesive, a glue gun or with a button.

# Holiday Spirit

I want to have a Christmas atmosphere in my living room, but I try to avoid the traditional red Christmas decorations. In this chapter I have used warm soft turquoise colours together with glitter and angel motifs as Christmas decorations.

You will find ideas like a gingerbread house made of cardboard and fabric that you can enjoy year after year. Miniature angels and purses will make cute presents for your friends. Small décor projects, gift ideas like homemade ribbons and decorations will create a cozy Christmas atmosphere in your home.

*Warm winter wishes*

# Winter Bunny

## INSTRUCTIONS
Read more about stuffed figures on page 4.
Fold a piece of fabric large enough for two rabbit shapes right sides together. Trace the rabbit from the pattern and remember to mark the opening. Sew around the rabbit and cut out.

Use a wooden stick or similar and turn the rabbit right sides out. Iron the rabbit and use the wooden stick to help you stuff it. When you are done stuffing it, use an iron to press the rabbit flat.

YOU WILL NEED:
Fabric
Paper wings (see page 5)
Toy stuffing
String for a hanger
Ribbons or paper rose for decorations

Pattern is on page 36

A

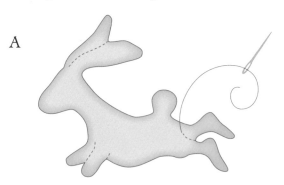

Stitch through the rabbit to make the dotted lines shown on the pattern (see Figure A).

Make wings as described on page 5. Attach a length of string to the body as a hanger so the rabbit will hang nicely.

A paper rose is used to decorate this rabbit.

# Mini Angel

### INSTRUCTIONS

Fold the skin fabric right sides together and trace the body, arms and legs from the pattern. Cut out and sew around the seam. Turn out and iron the parts. Iron under the seam allowance at the openings for legs and arms. Stuff the parts.

Place the legs inside the body and stitch. Stitch the arms to the body (see Figure A). Cut a strip of fabric approximately 11cm x 4cm (4¼ in x 1½ in). Fold the strip in half lengthwise and attach it around the angel's body with a couple of stitches at the back (see Figure B). Cut a piece of fabric for the skirt measuring 28cm x 10cm (11 in x 4 in), adding a seam allowance. Fold the piece right sides together widthwise and sew up the back seam. Iron under the seam allowances along the top and bottom edges of the skirt and stitch the bottom hem. Baste around the top of the skirt and gather it around the waist of the angel. Stitch it in place.

YOU WILL NEED:
Fabric for the skin
Fabric for the dress
Paper wings (see page 46)
Tilda hair or similar
Embroidery thread in the same colour as the hair
Toy stuffing
String for a hanger

*Pattern is on page 35*

Make the hair, face and paper wings as described on page 5. Attach a length of string as a hanger.

The angels can be decorated with glitter glue and Tilda patterned papers.

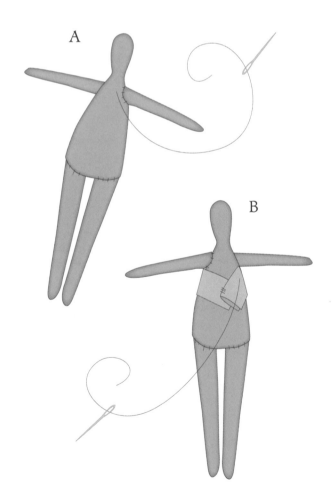

A

B

10

# Gift Ideas

## HOMEMADE RIBBONS

Make homemade ribbons by cutting strips of fabric the same width and sew them together for the desired length. Use a rotary cutter to make this easier. Finish the ribbons by sewing a zigzag stitch along the edges so they won't fray. Wind the ribbons onto Tilda wooden reels. You can find labels for the reels on page 46.

## GLASS CANDLE HOLDERS

Glass candle holders make lovely gifts. Here they are decorated with patterned silk paper and paper images. You can find equipment for making candles in craft stores.

## ROMANTIC SOAPS

The soaps are made of natural soap paste. You can add colour and fragrance to it, or leave it without additives if the gift is for someone with allergies. Wrap the soaps in cellophane and then in wrapping paper, parcel paper, fabric or similar. Finally, decorate them with stickers, paper images and embellishments before placing them in a decorated gift box.

# Decoration Ideas

## CARDBOARD CORNET

Make a cornet using decorated cardboard and glue. Use a quarter of a circle as a pattern for the cornet. Decorate the cornets with 3D stickers and ribbons. Attach a ribbon to use as a hanger with a stapler or brads.

## TREE DECORATIONS

Christmas decorations made out of small fluted tartlet tins look best if you can find old tins with some patina on them. Flea markets and garage sales would be a great place to look. If you can't find any, new ones will work as well.

Make a hole by placing the fluted edge of the tartlet tin down on a towel. Press the sharp point of some scissors against the tin until it breaks through. Twist the scissors to enlarge the hole slightly.

Make holes in the paper images using a hole punch and attach string as a hanger.

*Make your Christmas memorable and unique with distinctive tree decorations*

*You can enjoy an everlasting gingerbread house year after year ...*

# Everlasting Gingerbread House

YOU WILL NEED:
Cardboard for walls, roof and floor
Brown fabric for the walls
White fabric for the roof
Double-sided fusible web
Buttons and lace for decorations
Decorated paper for the interior
Windows and doors (see page 47)

*Pattern is on pages 41 – 43*

## INSTRUCTIONS

You will need to work carefully and accurately to make this house. Read through all the instructions before you begin. Making the window panes can be fiddly, but you can skip this step if you want to. If you do, just glue the windows to the house as they are shown on the pattern. You also won't need to cut openings for the windows or paper the inside of the house.

It is a good idea to use strong, but not too thick, cardboard. The back of a writing pad or the cardboard envelope from large photo paper would be perfect.

*Walls*

The pattern for the walls is in three parts: front wall (page 42), side wall (page 43) and back wall (page 42). The front and back walls are marked with a folding edge. Turn the pattern over along the folding edge to make sure you obtain the whole image. You also need two side walls.

Trace the walls onto cardboard and cut out using a utility knife and ruler. Also cut holes for the windows. To make the bay on the front wall, lightly score and then fold along the vertical lines on the pattern.

Place the walls face down next to each other. Glue the touching edges together with strong duct or plastic tape so the walls are connected, but can easily be folded (see Figure A).

Cut a strip of fabric slightly larger than the whole pattern. Iron fusible web to the wrong side of the fabric and pull off the paper. Place the fabric on the ironing board with the adhesive side up. Place the strip of wall pieces down on top.

Cut around the walls about 2–3mm (¹⁄₈ in) from the edge. Cut a notch by every corner. Fold the fabric towards the back of the walls and iron carefully. The fusible web will act as an adhesive (see Figure B). Be careful not to tighten the fabric too much so you can still fold the walls. Cut an x-shaped hole in the fabric for each window opening, fold the fabric around the edge and iron (see Figure C).Use tape as well if the fusible web isn't strong enough.

A

B

C

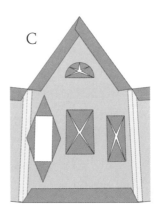

It's a good idea to paper the inside walls with decorated paper if you want to have open windows. Trace the walls onto the paper and cut 2–3mm (⅛ in) inside the line so the wallpaper is smaller than the actual walls. Glue the wallpaper to the actual walls (see Figure D).

*Floor*
The floor pattern is also marked with a folding edge and should be doubled. Make the floor in the same way as the walls, with fabric and decorative paper. The slot along the back edge is there to put light inside the house when you are done.
Fold and bend the house so it will fit the floor. The walls are supposed to lean inwards slightly (see picture opposite). Use a glue gun and attach the walls to the floor one at the time. Hold the walls until the adhesive has dried. Also glue together the last two vertical edges (see Figure E).

*Roof*
The roof pattern is marked with a folding edge and must be doubled. Score along the folding edge so the roof can be folded easily. Cut out a rectangle on the front edge of the roof for the bay as marked with the dotted line. Cover the roof the same way as the walls, but with white fabric.

Glue the roof to the house with the glue gun and make sure the notch in the roof is over the bay (see Figure F). The bay pattern should also be doubled, and scored so it can be folded along the folding line. Cover and attach (see Figure G).

*Windows and door*
You will find the windows and door on page 47. Make copies or scan and print them onto slightly thicker matt photo paper. It's a good idea to have two copies in case you make a mistake. Start to cut out the windows using a utility knife and ruler. Then, if you wish, carefully cut out the window and door panes. Glue the windows and door in place.

Glue buttons onto the roof and lace around the roof edge with a glue gun if you want to decorate the house. Add some glitter glue to the window and door frames.

D
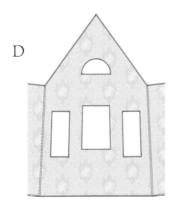

E
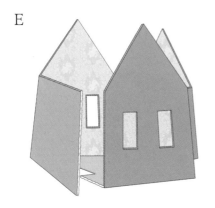

F
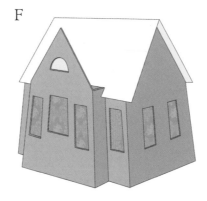

G
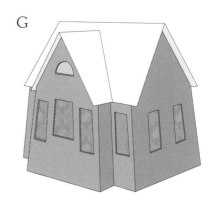

# Purse

## INSTRUCTIONS

Cut a strip measuring 20cm x 34cm (8 in x 13½ in) and a strip measuring 3cm x 34cm (1⅛ in x 13½ in) for the outside of the purse. Cut a strip measuring 22.5cm x 34cm (9 in x 13½ in) for the lining. Also cut a strip measuring 80cm x 7cm (31½ in x 2¾ in) for the ruffle. Add seam allowance to all of the measurements.

Fold under the seam allowances on the short sides of the ruffle. Fold and iron the strip in half lengthwise. Tack (baste) along the open side and gather the ruffle until it is 34cm (13½ in) long.

Bond the interfacing to the wrong side of the thin strip for the purse. Place the thin and the wide strips for the outside of the purse right sides together with the ruffle in between, and sew along the edge (see Figure A). Sew the lining strip to the raw edge of the thin strip.

Fold the purse and lining right sides together and sew along the open side (see Figure B). Refold the purse so that the seam is in the middle and sew the raw edges at the top and bottom closed, leaving an opening in the lining (see Figure C).

Turn the purse right sides out and push the lining down into the purse. Iron the purse and then sew closely around the top edge so the lining will stay in place. Attach a ribbon as a carrying strap. Decorate with buttons if you want to.

YOU WILL NEED:
Fabric for the purse
Fabric for the lining
Iron-on fusible interfacing
Ribbon for the strap
Buttons for decorations

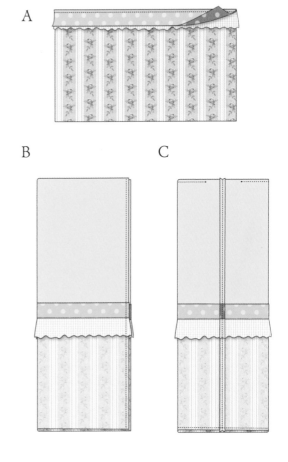

A

B          C

# Red and White Christmas

The kitchen is decorated in red and white and the Christmas workshop has started. Advent calendar gifts are hanging from a wreath above the table so presents can be opened every morning with breakfast.

Presents for friends and family are ready and beautifully wrapped with homemade Christmas cards and notes.

# Santa Claus

## INSTRUCTIONS

Each of the patterns for the body, jacket and pants are divided in two parts. Put the parts together, matching points A and B.

### Body

Cut two pieces of fabric for the skin and two pieces for the hat. Use the pattern to position the parts together along the slanting dotted line (see Figure A). Sew the parts for the hat to the body as shown in Figure B.

Place the two parts right sides together, trace the pattern and sew around the shape (see Figure C). Cut out, turn right sides out and iron the body. Fold fabric for the arms and legs right sides together. Trace, sew around, cut out, turn right sides out and iron. Fold under the edges on the body and arms. Stuff the pieces. Stitch the opening at the bottom of the body closed.

### Legs, boots and pants

On this Santa the legs should be sewn to the pants before the pants are attached to the body. Notice that the pants pattern is marked with a folding edge and should be doubled. Place the two parts for the pants right sides together (see Figure D).

YOU WILL NEED:
Fabric for the skin
Fabric for the jacket and hat
Fabric for the pants
Fabric for the bag and boots
Fabric for the bunny head
Fabric for the candy cane
Tilda hair or similar
Tilda loops or buttons
Wadding (batting)
Broad ribbon for decoration

*Pattern is on pages 36 – 40*

Make the boots, following the instructions for legs on page 4. After you have stuffed them, sew straight stitches across the front seams, using contrast thread, to make the laces.

Fold the pants so the seams lay over each other. Then sew the inside leg seams (see Figure E).

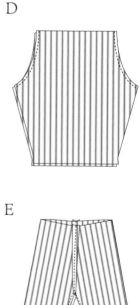

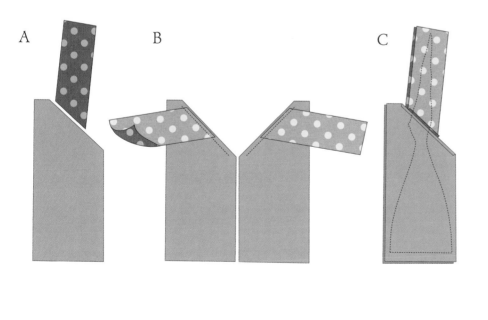

A          B          C          D

E

Turn right sides out, fold the raw edges under and iron the pants. Baste around each leg opening and place the legs inside the openings to fit. Stitch the legs to the pants.

Cut two strips of fabric for the leg cuffs measuring 5cm x 11cm (2 in x 4¼ in) seam allowance included. Iron under 1cm (³⁄₈ in) on each long edge and attach the cuffs around the bottom of the pants (see Figure F). Stitch the pants to Santa's waist.

Make the arms, following the instructions on page 4. Then attach them under the neck on each side of the Santa (see Figure G).

*Jacket*
Note that the jacket pattern is marked with a folding edge and should be doubled. Cut one piece of fabric using the outer folding edge and another using the inner folding edge, so one of the pieces is wider (see Figure H). Fold and sew a tuck in the wider piece for the front buttoned edge so the pieces are the same size (see Figure I). Place the two parts right sides together and sew the shoulder seams. Sew on the sleeves as shown in Figure J.

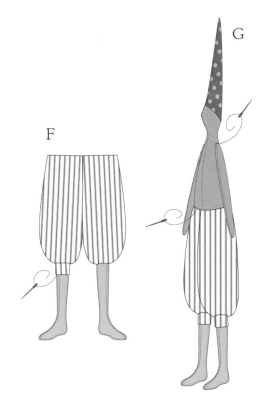

Fold up the large seam allowance at the bottom of the jacket right sides together. Trace and stitch around the scalloped edge approximately 2mm (¹⁄₈ in) from the fold (see Figure K). Cut out the scalloped edge and cut a notch to the seam in between each scallop. Use a wooden stick to turn the scallops out and iron.

You can sew the seam allowance above the scallops if necessary. Fold the jacket right sides together and sew the underarm and side seams on the jacket (see Figure L).

### Beard

Make the face as described on page 5 before you make the beard. Then make a bundle of Tilda hair or similar for a beard by twisting the hair around a small piece of cardboard or something similar measuring about 12cm (4¾ in). Thread a piece of hair through the bundle (see Figure N). Tie the bundle around the Santa's head and pull the knot up a little to make the beard go around each side of the head (see Figure O).

Stitch the top edge of the beard to the head before you cut the bundle at the bottom. If you wish, you can use a glue gun to attach the hair at the bottom.

### Loop

You can sew a loop if you want to hang the Santa somewhere. Cut a strip of fabric measuring 5cm x 15cm (2 in x 6 in). Iron under 1cm (³/₈ in) on each end and iron the strip in half lengthwise. Sew along the open side. Cut a piece of a wide ribbon, long enough to be attached diagonally around the Santa's head.

Stitch the loop to the neck and then the ribbon around the head (see Figure P). It is important to attach the ribbon high enough at the front so as not to cover the face and then cross it over at the back of the neck.

Turn out the jacket and iron (see Figure M). Dress the Santa in the jacket. The neck opening is quite tight so get a good grip of the hat and pull the head through carefully. Fold under the raw edge around the neck opening and stitch it in place if you want to.

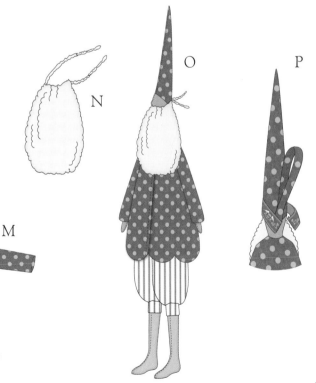

L

M

N

O

P

*Bag*

Cut a piece of fabric big enough to take the bag twice, adding a seam allowance. Iron under the seam allowance across the top of the bag. Sew a ribbon to the edge if you want to. Fold the bag right sides together and sew around the raw edges.

Turn out and iron the bag. Stuff it with some wadding (batting).

Fold fabric for the candy cane right sides together, trace the shape from the pattern and sew around it. Use a wooden stick or similar to help to turn out and stuff it.

Sew the bunny head as the bunny on page 9. It is not necessary to close the raw edges. Use a glue gun or stitch the bunny to the bag (see Figure Q).

Sew frog fastenings or buttons to the jacket (see picture on page 24). Sew or glue the bag under the arm.

# Little Santa Girl

## INSTRUCTIONS

Sew together a strip of hat fabric and a strip of skin fabric. Fold the strip right sides together. Trace the pattern and sew around. Cut, turn out and stuff the body.

Sew the arms, legs and dress in the same way as for the Mini Angel on page 10. Make the hair as described on page 5, but make sure the fringe stops where the hat begins and only attach a little bit of hair underneath the edge of the hat before you attach the hair bundles on each side of the head. Make the face as described on page 5.

YOU WILL NEED:
Fabric for the skin
Fabric for the dress and hat
Embroidery thread in the same colour as the hair
Tilda hair or similar
Toy stuffing

*Pattern is on page 35*

# Food Gifts

These are not recipes, but ideas on how to wrap food gifts nicely.

Red and white striped ribbon and gift boxes are beautiful for dark chocolate colours.

A decorated marzipan ring cake is a perfect Christmas present for neighbours and friends.

A pile of macaroon tarts on a cute plate decorated with ribbons can be wrapped in cellophane as a lovely gift.

Homemade (or shop-bought) chocolates would be a great gift wrapped in cellophane paper and ribbon decorations. Place the chocolates in a gift box on a paper doily.

The purse on page 21, sewn in red and white candy colours, and the cornet on page 14 make perfect candy bags.

# Angel Stocking

## INSTRUCTIONS

### Stocking

The pattern is in three parts. Put together the two parts for the foot, matching points A and B. Measure 23cm (9 in) up and then trace the stocking top. Draw two lines connecting the top and foot (see Figure A).

Cut out two full pieces of the stocking and two matching pieces of wadding (batting). Add more than enough seam allowance on all edges, avoid cutting the scalloped edge and make sure you have matching left and right pieces. Then cut out two pieces of lining fabric from the stocking pattern, ending at the broken line. Also cut two contrasting edges from the part of the pattern above the broken line. Pin the wadding (batting) to the wrong side of the stocking fabric. Sew the contrasting edges to the top of the lining edges.

Place the main fabric pieces right sides together with the lining, top edges aligned. Trace and sew along the scalloped edge (see Figure B). Cut out the scalloped edge and cut notches in the seam between each scallop. Tweak the scallops back and forth a little so the fabric loosens along the seam.

Open out the stocking parts that are sewn together and place the two pieces right sides together. Fold the scalloped edge towards the wadding (batting). Sew around the stocking, making sure to start and stop at the ends of the scallop seam (see Figure B). Also be sure to leave an opening for turning along the back edge of the stocking (see Figure C).

Turn right sides out. Use a wooden stick to turn out the scallops. Push the lining into the stocking and fold the contrasting edge down so it is visible. Iron the stocking.

If you are patient, you can quilt the stocking by hand. Place a piece of cardboard inside it to avoid sewing the front and back together. Make a loop the same way as for the Santa (see page 27) and stitch on the inside of the stocking.

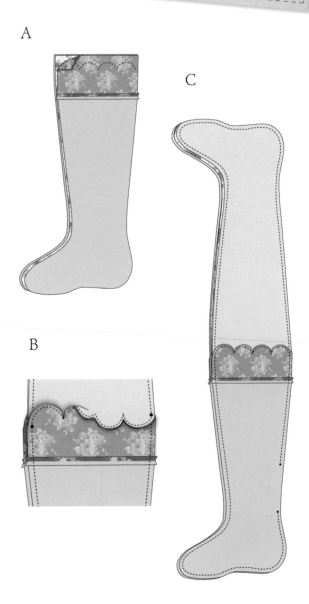

A

B

C

Fill your stocking with
gifts fit for angels

*Wings*
Fold the fabric for the wings right sides together
and trace two wings from the pattern. Sew around
(see Figure D).

Cut, turn out and iron the wings. Sew stitches to
match the broken lines on the pattern. Use a wooden
stick or similar to stuff the wings. You could press
the wings with a flat iron after they have been
stuffed. Fold under the raw edges and stitch the
wings to the stocking (see Figure D).

D

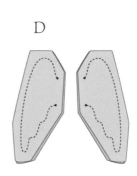

E

# Patterns

Add seam allowances to all patterns unless otherwise stated in the instructions. Broken lines indicate openings, seams or lines for matching the pattern pieces. ES means extra seam allowance and marks openings where it is important to have more than enough seam allowance.

Scan and print out or photocopy the patterns to use. All patterns are shown at actual size and do not need to be enlarged. The illustrations are for private use only.

## Mini Angel and Little Santa Girl

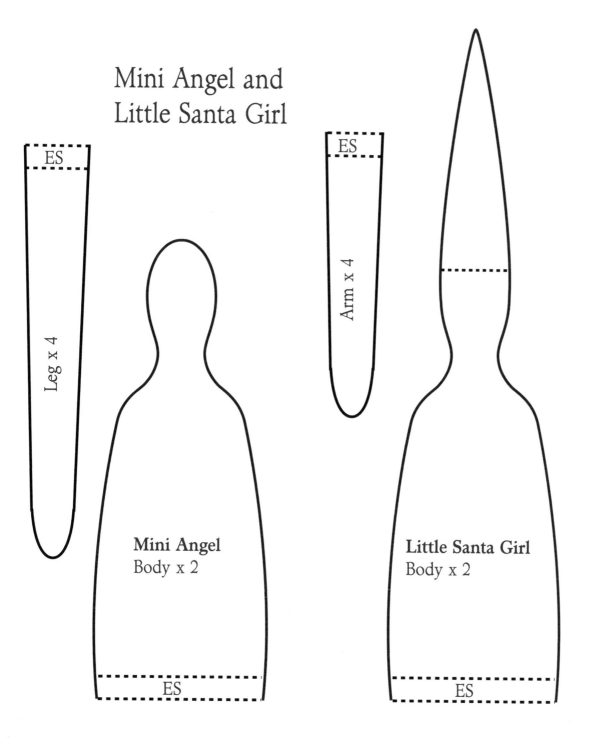

ES

Leg x 4

**Mini Angel**
Body x 2

ES

ES

Arm x 4

**Little Santa Girl**
Body x 2

ES

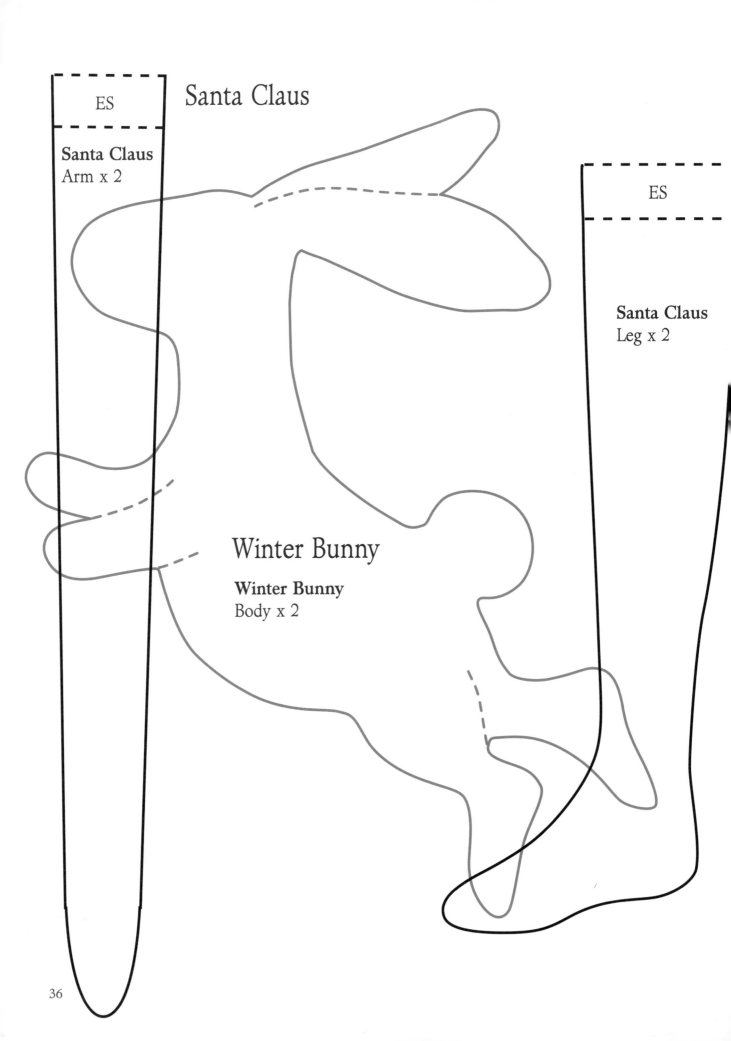

ES

**Santa Claus**
Arm x 2

Santa Claus

ES

**Santa Claus**
Leg x 2

Winter Bunny

**Winter Bunny**
Body x 2

ES

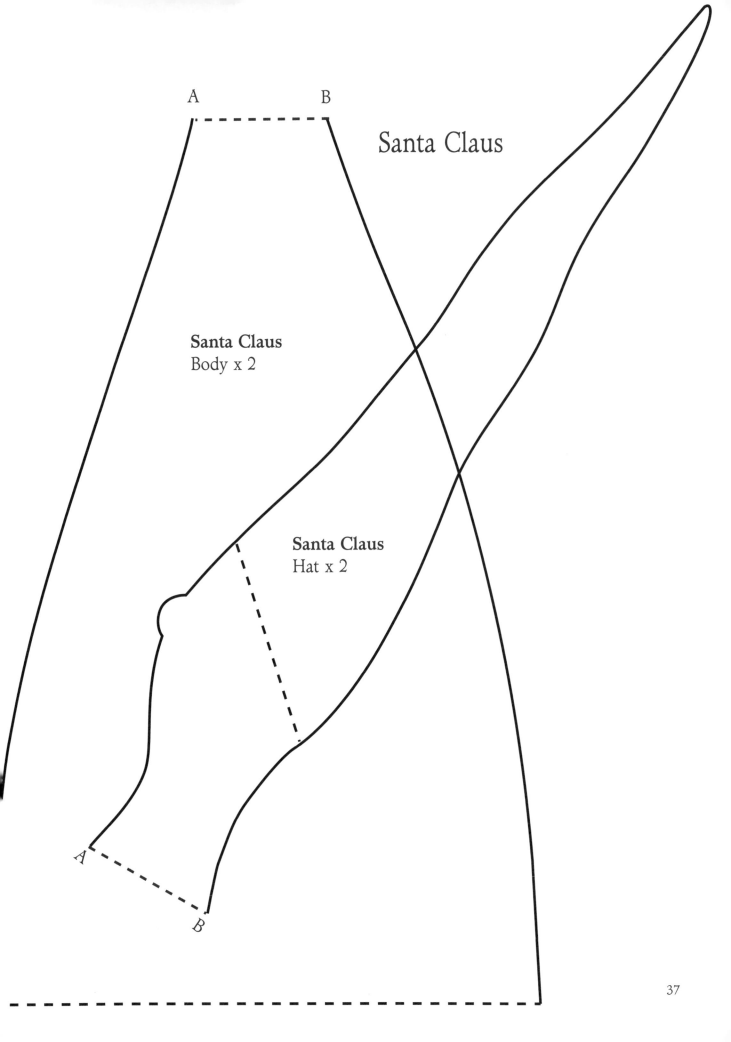

A    B

Santa Claus

**Santa Claus**
Body x 2

**Santa Claus**
Hat x 2

*A*

*B*

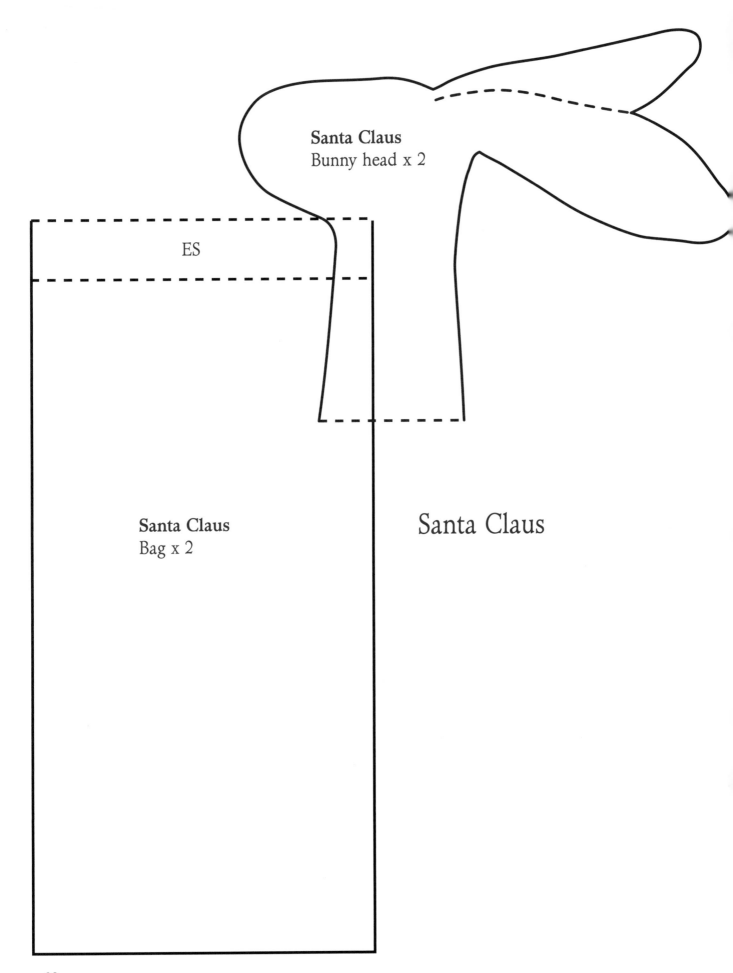

**Santa Claus**
Bunny head x 2

ES

**Santa Claus**
Bag x 2

Santa Claus

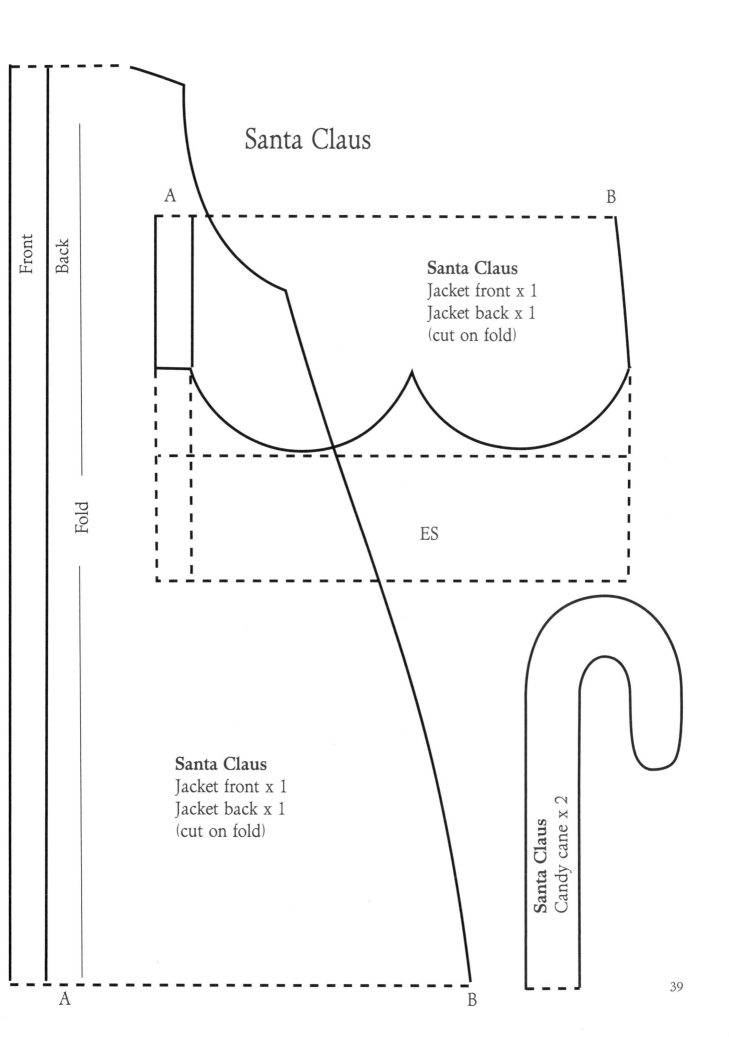

Santa Claus

Front

Back

Fold

A

B

**Santa Claus**
Jacket front x 1
Jacket back x 1
(cut on fold)

ES

**Santa Claus**
Jacket front x 1
Jacket back x 1
(cut on fold)

**Santa Claus**
Candy cane x 2

A

B

39

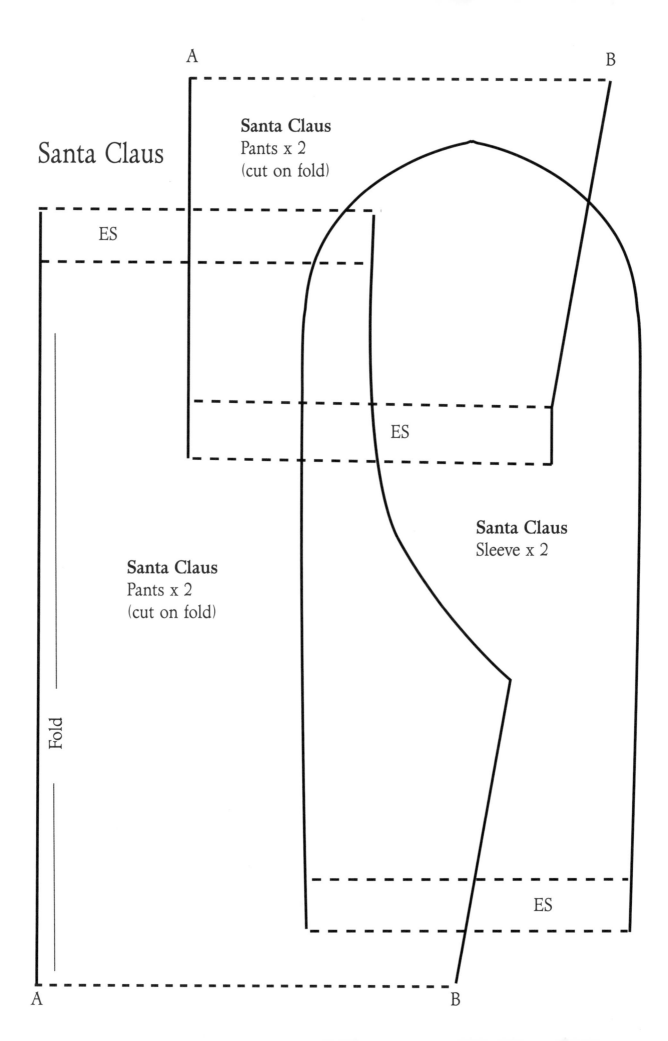

A

B

Santa Claus

**Santa Claus**
Pants x 2
(cut on fold)

ES

ES

**Santa Claus**
Pants x 2
(cut on fold)

**Santa Claus**
Sleeve x 2

Fold

ES

A

B

# Gingerbread House

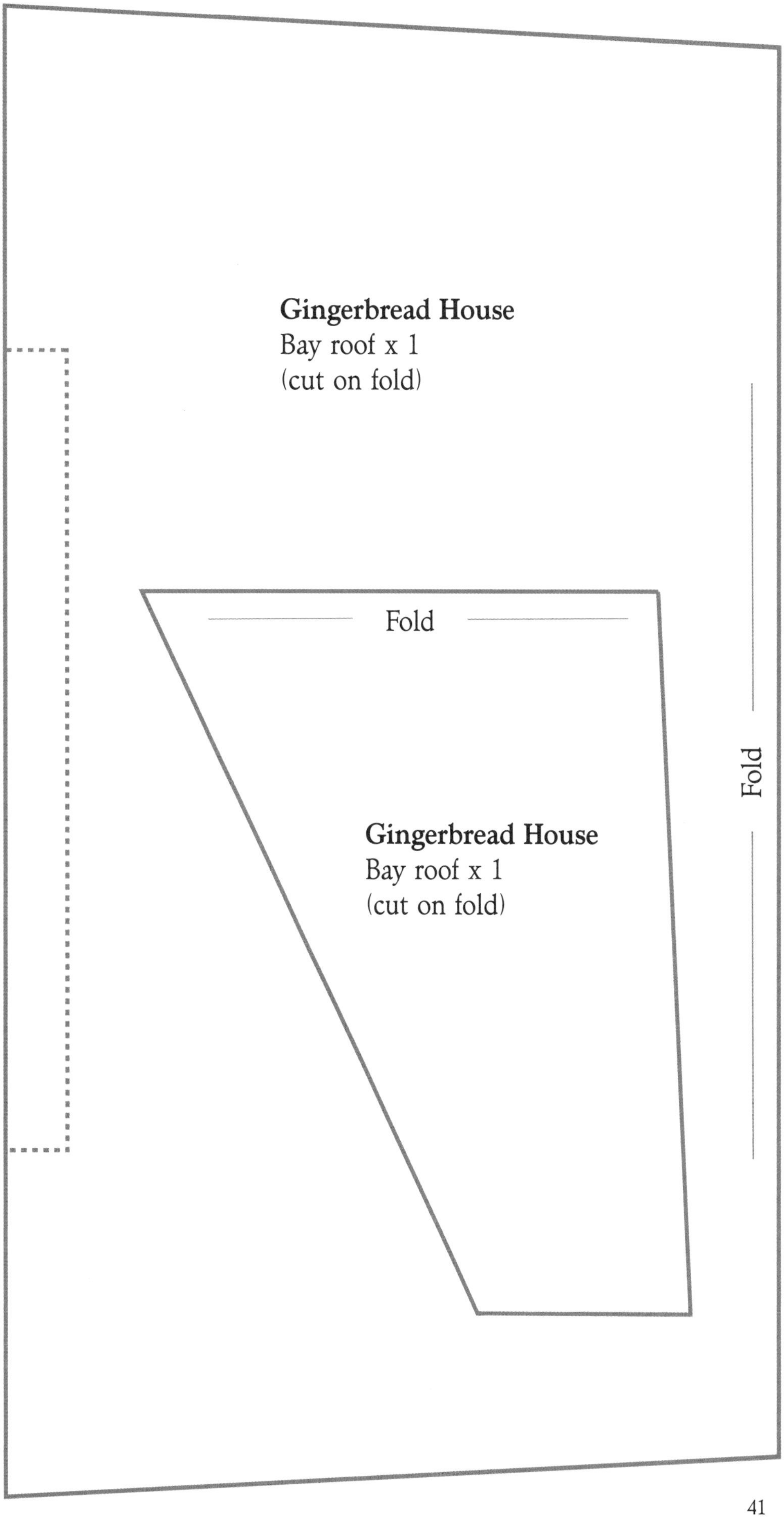

**Gingerbread House**
Bay roof x 1
(cut on fold)

Fold

Fold

**Gingerbread House**
Bay roof x 1
(cut on fold)

# Gingerbread House

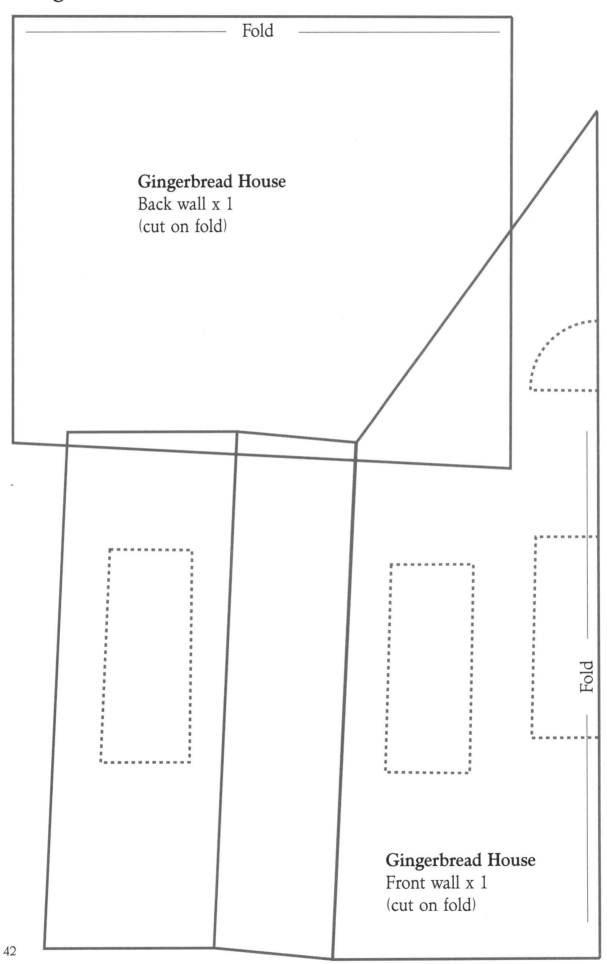

Fold

**Gingerbread House**
Back wall x 1
(cut on fold)

Fold

**Gingerbread House**
Front wall x 1
(cut on fold)

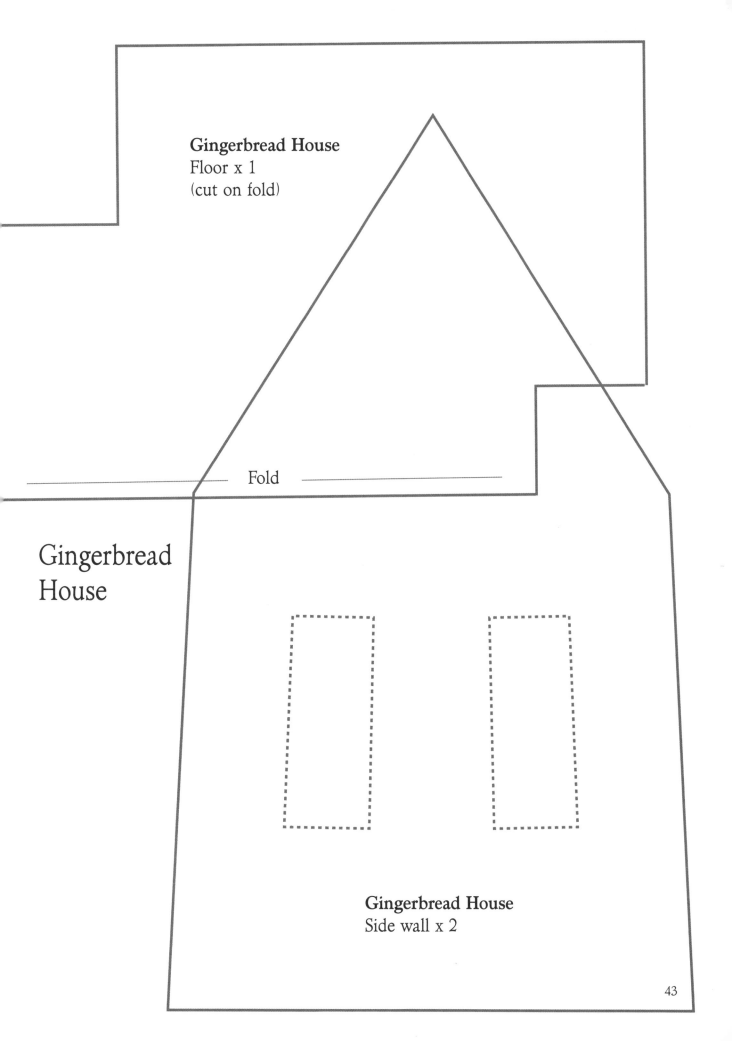

**Gingerbread House**
Floor x 1
(cut on fold)

Fold

Gingerbread
House

**Gingerbread House**
Side wall x 2

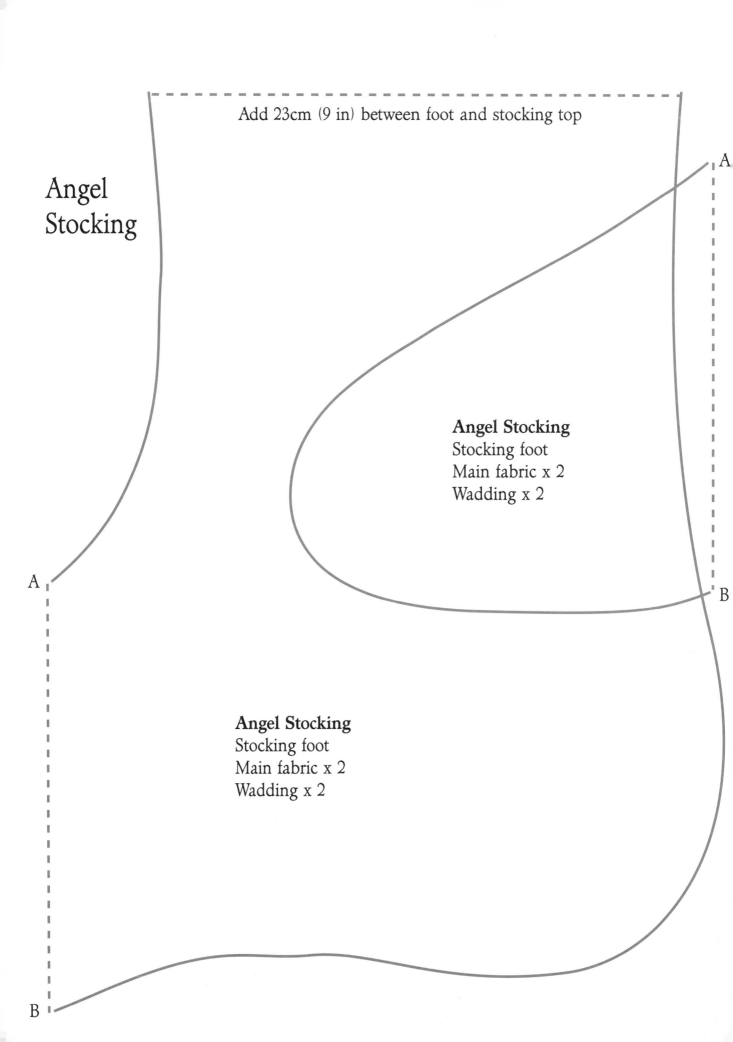

Angel
Stocking

Add 23cm (9 in) between foot and stocking top

A

**Angel Stocking**
Stocking foot
Main fabric x 2
Wadding x 2

A

B

**Angel Stocking**
Stocking foot
Main fabric x 2
Wadding x 2

B

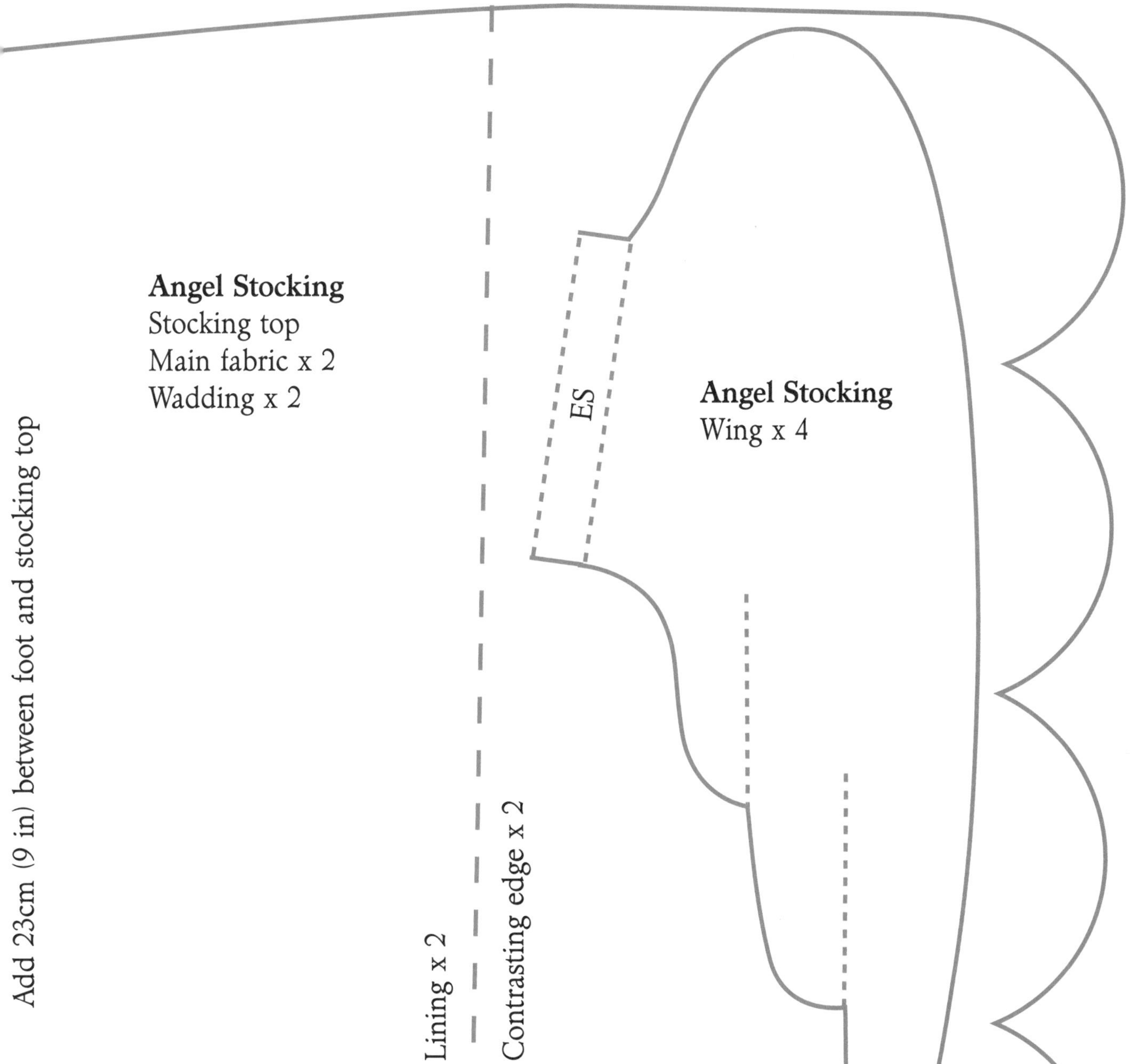

Add 23cm (9 in) between foot and stocking top

**Angel Stocking**
Stocking top
Main fabric x 2
Wadding x 2

**Angel Stocking**
Wing x 4

*ES*

Lining x 2

Contrasting edge x 2

Angel Stocking

Wings for the Mini Angel

Wooden wheel décor for
the homemade ribbons

Wings for the Winter Bunny

# Windows and door for the Gingerbread House

## Props

LandRomAntikk
Tornerose
Home and Cottage

## Acknowledgments

Sølvi Dos Santos for her great pictures
Ingrid Skansaar for beautiful styling
Tom Undhjem for repro
Karin Mundal and Cappelen Damm

# Suppliers

## UK

Panduro Hobby
Westway House
Transport Avenue
Brentford
Middlesex TW8 9HF
Tel: 020 8566 1680
trade@panduro.co.uk
www.pandurohobby.co.uk

Coast and Country
Crafts & Quilts
8 Sampson Gardens
Ponsanooth
Cornwall TR3 7RS
Tel: 01872 863894
www.coastandcountry
crafts.co.uk

Fred Aldous Ltd.
37 Lever Street
Manchester M1 1LW
Tel: 08707 517301
www.fredaldous.co.uk

The Fat Quarters
5 Choprell Road
Blackhall Mill
Newcastle NE17 7TN
Tel: 01207 565728
www.thefatquarters.co.uk

The Sewing Bee
52 Hillfoot Street
Dunoon
Argyll PA23 7DT
Tel: 01369 706879
www.thesewingbee.co.uk

Puddle Crafts
3 Milltown Lodge
Sandpit
Termonfeckin
County Louth
Ireland
Tel: 00353 87 355 0219
www.puddlecrafts.co.uk

Threads and Patches
48 Aylesbury Street
Fenny Stratford
Bletchley
Milton Keynes MK2 2BU
Tel: 01908 649687
www.threadsand
patches.co.uk

## USA

Coats and Clark USA
PO Box 12229
Greenville
SC29612-0229
Tel: 0800 648 1479
www.coatsandclark.com

Connecting Threads
13118 NE 4th Street
Vancouver
WA 9884
www.connectingthreads.com

eQuilter.com
5455 Spine Road, Suite E
Boulder
CO 80301
www.equilter.com

Hamels Fabrics
5843 Lickman Road
Chilliwack
British Columbia
V2R 4B5
www.hamelsfabrics.com

Keepsake Quilting
Box 1618 Center Harbor
NH 03226
www.keepsakequilting.com

The Craft Connection
21055 Front Street
PO Box 1088
Onley
VA 23418
www.craftconn.com

# Index